Broken Hearts Do Heal

Lady D

Speaks on the Bitter and
Sweet of Being in Love

JCV Communications
Nashville, Tennessee

Broken Hearts Do Heal

Published by JCV Communications
Box 280391
Nashville, TN 37228
ISBN — 1-893078-05-1

Copyright 1999 by Regina Vincent Clark

All rights reserved. No part of this publication may be reproduced, stored in a retrieval system, or transmitted, in any form, or by any means, electronic, mechanical, photocopying, recording, performed or otherwise, without the written permission of the publisher, JCV Communications.

Graphic Design by: Debbie Moore
Cover Photo by: Regina Clark
Printing by: Classic Printing, Nashville, TN

For further information, contact
JCV Communications, Box 280391, Nashville, TN 37228
or JCV2010@aol.com.

*Dedicated to my brother,
Milton L. Vincent,
a "tough and tender soul,"
April 10, 1947 – August 6, 1999.*

Contents

Prologue 9
Learning the Rules in the Game of Life......... 11
Never Yes, Never No..12
Because..13
With Tenderness, I Think of You 14
Uhmnnnn……...15
It's Time 16
A One Night Stand 17
You Touched Me 18
Naturally So…...19
A New Awakening 20

Physical Fitness: Poetic Exercise for the Heart

Physical Fitness..22
Tremors 23
Foxes...24
The Love We Make 25
Elmer's Glue 26
A Day At A Time..27
Something About U and I...28
If You Were To Love Me 29
And If I Am To Love You..30
Lasting Memories 31
Erasing Memories...32
A Split Second 33
A Very Sophisticated Problem 34
Pain Needs No Title 35
Love Redefined 36
More..37
Quick Fixes 36
Einstein & Frankenstein — On Love 39
Letting Go 40

Loving, Hurting, and Loving Even More 41
In Thin Air 42
Too Much Distance, Not Enough Time 43
A Love Revelation 44
Just Because I Guess 45
My Foolish Ways.. 46
Doing Without You 47
Necessary Needs.. 48
His Eyes 49
A Certain Feeling On A Certain Day... 50
Wondering 51
Not At All Surprised 52
Internal Struggles.. 53
Loveless Love 54
The Choice Is Yours 55
Inside 56
This Time It Was For Real 57
Kindly Tell Me So 58
Loving You To Death 59
Tears In the Night... 60
A Time To Feel My Pain.. 61
Oooohhh!!! 63
I Wanted To…. 64
What We Had Before 65
I'm Out of Your Life, You Don't Deserve My Love........................ 66

Taking The Load Off Baby

The Sisters At Selena's Salon 69
Getting Over 71
A Kept Woman 72
Do You Know???? 73
My X, My Ace, My Deuce and Three Quarters Yet........................ 74
Or Is It? 75
The Lie You Told Last Night.. 76
Why Must We Lie?.. 78
The Truth Is.. 80
Don't Come Here With That 81
Mad As Hell... 83
Gutterland... 84

Like A Man 86
Not So Great Expectations..87
The Things We Do….and Don't 89
Time Just Ain't The Same 91
Terry's Response 93

Healing: The Bitter Can Sometimes Be Very Sweet!!

Tears of Joy 96
Special Attraction 97
The User's Manual for A Healthy Relationship..............98
Friendship..99
Sunshine...100
Always There 101
Platonic Energy 102
Reasoning 103
A Wish, A Fantasy, A Dream Come True 104
Couldn't See the Forest 105
Memories of You 106
Your Broken Heart...107
Habit 108
Is There a Prescription?..109
Acknowledgement 110
Epilogue 111

Prologue

Don't be shocked, stunned, or amazed at the confession I am about to make. In fact you might find yourself one day making a similar confession. I am afraid of falling in love. The idea of falling anywhere frightens me just a bit. I have considered jumping from an airplane to skydive — but I shiver at the thought of falling. As a youngster, I jumped a lot — from high places, in games like Mother May I, and just through the simple exertion of excess energy. But I never liked falling, which I did my fair share of.

Today, when I think of falling in love, I think of the many times I have fallen, and the pain I've felt. Yes, there was always something good about falling in love. I have enjoyed the feeling of having someone on my mind all the time. I reflect back on the unselfish state of living that falling in love brings — that willingness to go the extra mile. There is a glow that invades one's body when one is "in love." Love is sweet. Love is comforting. Love is sustaining. But falling in love can be and is scary sometimes.

An unknown author writes in the poem "Risk It:" ...*to love is to risk not being loved in return, to live is to risk dying, to hope is to risk despair, to try is to risk failure, but risks must be taken; because the greatest hazard in life is to risk nothing. The person who risks nothing, does nothing, has nothing, and is nothing. He may avoid suffering and sorrow, but he simply cannot learn, feel, change, grow, love, live. Only a person who risks is free.*" And that, my friend, sums it up for "Broken Hearts Do Heal." Written as a response to the song, "How Do You Mend A Broken Heart," this collection of poetry can't tell you how — but through the bitter and the sweet of poems included, just know that "Broken Hearts Do Heal." Know that if you've fallen in love once you are likely to do so again. Know that when the heart is broken, it does mend. And know that there is something good, something marvelous, something indescribable about falling in love. Enjoy!!!

—Lady D

Learning the Rules in the Game of Life

As I approach forty I am
Beginning to learn that
Life can't be taken too seriously.
That being in love should never be
Thought of in terms of permanently.
That loved ones, lovers, friends, and foes,
Will, in your life, come…
And they'll go.
Nothing lasts forever,
And broken hearts do heal,
In the game of life, play long enough,
And you will get to deal.
It doesn't matter if you're twenty or forty, or
Sixty or so….Don't play the game too seriously,
For all too swiftly, the game of life will let you go.

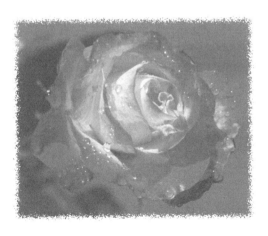

Never Yes, Never No

He loves me? He loves me not?
He loves me? He loves me not?
Does it really matter? He gives it his best shot!
Were it not for the question never being answered,
I certainly would not have known the difference.
But the question was always asked,
The answer was never "yes,"
Nor was it "no."
Cause like he said a million times,
Love is not what you say,
But what you show.

Because

I could hardly drink my tea or
Eat my breakfast
Because this smile
Kept appearing
In my face,
Making it difficult
To take in food…smiling
Involuntarily
Because I kept thinking of you and
When we first met
Because
It's been a whole year now and we're still together
Because you are such a very special person
And needless to say
Because I love you.

With Tenderness, I Think of You

When I think of you, it is unquestionably with tenderness
For that is you.
The way you love and make love.
It is always with tenderness
Unquestionably.
Thus, therefore, and forevermore —
When I think of you
Your
Tenderness, Love, and Gentleness
Emanate through and through.

Uhmnn.....

I sure would like to be made love to
To be taken in and warmly embraced
Sweetly caressed and very passionately
Unhesitatingly and most completely,
Made love to……
By someone who is in love with me.

It's Time

It's time for me to be dined and wined,
And swept off my feet.
It's been far too long
Since I had a decent man in my life.
And being held by one has
Crossed my mind lately
More than once or twice.
It's time for me to be held tightly
Rightly,
All through the night,
Time for me to know love again,
From a loving, caring, decent man.
Far too many moments
I've gone without....
Too many pleasurable moments
Have been pushed aside and forgotten about....
It's time for me to
Live again....
And enjoy the pleasures of life
That come from
Loving
A Real Man.

A One Night Stand

I was looking for a one night stand
I found that just one night I could not stand!!!
How dare your love be so good!!!

You Touched Me

You touched me
And my heart skipped
Not just one beat
But nine or ten,
There was nothing physical
Yet you touched me,
With your kindness
Tenderness
Your Gentle-MAN-ness,
You touched me
And I immediately
Became your friend.
My heart skipped not just one beat
But nine or ten,
Can't wait to have you
Touch Me Again!!!!

Naturally So……

Do you ever get icy chills every now and then
A not so cheap thrill and sometimes a sweet made-love-to
Feeling…..when you think of the two of us together???

A New Awakening

When I saw you
I experienced
A New Awakening
Within in my soul.
Portions of me
Became anew
When I saw you…
When I saw you
I experienced joy,
And hope, and love…
And strength, and pleasure, and
Power, and peace.
When I saw you.
When I saw you
I experienced a new
And very Satisfying
Awakening.

PHYSICAL FITNESS:
POETIC EXERCISE FOR THE HEART

Physical Fitness

Neither of us were looking for love
or any emotional tie of the sort.
We made sure of that.
By keeping some 440 — relay???
Spring cross country like distance
From one another.
It was an exercise in physical fitness —
When we could...
We were always careful to *warm up*
And *cool down*.
On the other hand,
There were times we couldn't
Or didn't ...
Keep that certain distance
From one another...Those times
When the physical was mightier
And more electromagnetically charged
Than the mental...
and emotional restraint.
We each claimed to have so much of.
So even though we would make love.
Good love. We both knew that
Neither of us were looking for love.
We concluded that we were physically fit.
Kissed one another goodbye...
And held on to memories never to be forgotten...
The exercise was complete
The gym closed for the night
It was a physical workout
And a mental flight.

Tremors

After we have made
Passionate love…
Which more times than not causes
The midnight skies to light up—
I feel that I've come through
Some off-the-Richter-scale
Lovequake….
With aftershocks
And tremors
And pleasant memories
That last for
Days and days……

Foxes

It's ironic that the hounds were chasing me
I was chasing you.
Apparently, the fox hunt is relative,
Like many things in life.

Physical Fitness: Poetic Exercise for the Heart

The Love We Make

I love the love we make,
Especially when made before the
Morning dawn breaks,
Right before the sun brightens the sky,
The love we make just gets me high—
Off the planet and into the clouds,
Away from my fears, my sorrows, my doubts,
The love we make does all that to me,
It's powerful enough to make the blind see,
The love we make, makes me love
You with all my heart
The love we make makes a
Hell of a Love!!!!

Elmer's Glue

Okay, so I am hooked on you
Stuck on your loving like Elmer's glue
Missing you and wanting you
And fantasizing too.
Okay it's real
This feeling that I feel
This feeling of being hooked on you.
Think about you all the time
Morning, noon and night
You are on my mind.
You've consumed my body
I have no sense of time
Hooked on you and out of my mind,
Stuck on you like the early morning dew,
Yes there is precipitation
And yes you make me sweat too
Oh I know I gotta find something else to do…
Can't move through life being stuck on you.
I feel a psychological traffic jam
When I think of you
Stand still in my tracks like I'm standing in glue.
And fail to pay the bills sometimes when they come due…
So get ready my brother —
The heart and the brain are developing a strategic coup,
To rescue my body — my mind too
Can't afford to go through these changes being
Stuck on you.

A Day At A Time

When I wake up in the middle of the night,
Yours are the arms I long to hold me real tight.
Your body I wish were next to mine,
Your heart and mine keeping time.
Then I think of how short life is,
And I wish that you were here,
So that we could share more of life's gifts,
Life's pleasures, Its good and bad times.
It's not what you want
You've told me too many times.
A day, a step, a second at a time.
Play it by ear…..your favorite line.
But I wanted more, I won't deny it.
The beginning, the middle, I wanted it
All right up to the end.
All I ever asked was that you just say when,
Of course, nobody's love should be so strong.

Something About U and I

There was something about U
Perhaps your smile
Or was it that glow in your I's
That made me smile such a long while.
There was something that warmed my heart,
Quickened its beat
And made my feet
Dance to a beat
Of gentleness and happiness
And so much pleasure.
Perhaps U didn't notice
I tried to be discreet
Which is nearly impossible
When swept off your feet.
And made to feel so complete
Could'a been that smile
Or maybe those I's,
It was definitely U
Doin' what U do.

If You Were To Love Me

If you were to love me
Would you love me right?
Would you hold me close
And squeeze me real tight?
Would you take my hand
And walk with me any hour of the night?
If you were to love me,
Would you love me right?

If you were to love me,
Would you kiss me tenderly?
Would you whisper in my ear
Sweet words I'd love to hear?
Would you laugh with me
Cry with me, walk with me, fly with me?
Consider growing old and one day
Even die with me....
If you were to love me
Could I count on you being near?

If you were to love me
Would you make this love last?
Would you look more to the promise of our future
And less at the pain of our past?
Would you be my best friend,
Thru the thick and the thin?
If you were to love me
Now is when you should begin!!

And If I Am To Love You.....

If I am to love you, I have to also touch you,
To reach out and feel you — to know that you
Are there no matter where you are....I have to feel your pain,
Walk in your rain and enjoy the sunshine that makes
You smile....Let me be a witness to your triumphs, your trials,
Enlighten me on the miles you've walked,
The joy you've brought, I have to know you....I have to
Feel you...touch you... and not dare conceal you....and
If for example you were to take ill I'd want my love to
Somehow heal you...And the way you touch me
Should have a way of making me touch others
It should make me a better person.
A more loving person
A person growing and growing and growing,
But never getting too big and never thinking too small,
That is what I want from this experience many call love,
This is what I want to have if I am to love you.

Lasting Memories

We made the kind of memories
That never are forgotten,
They stand the test of time
Memories that are cherished, envied by the masses.
The kind that make you sweat in the night
But sometimes cause you to smile and folks to
Wonder what in the world could be on your mind.
The memories you count on
When Father Time steps in,
When you yourself wonder if you're
Com'in, or Go'in where and when
The memories we made are one of a kind
Memories that lovingly rejuvenate my body and mind.

Erasing Memories

Everywhere your name appeared
I fervently erased
Every letter, momento, memory of you,
I tried to replace.
The pictures are gone
The slates are clean
Except for those places
Where memories of you were
Deeply etched. Forever engraved.
Places deep within my heart.
Permanently inked deep in my soul.

A Split Second

Did you feel it?
That split second of ecstasy
When our souls merged.
When I was you and you were me.
It was just for a second
Though it still feels like
Eternity.
It was hotter than fire,
More shocking than electricity.
It was love. It was life.
It was you and me.

A Very Sophisticated Problem

I stop and think how wrong
I am to feel what I feel yet,
I've not been successful in fighting my feelings.
And that is wrong too. I guess
I've been too realistic in knowing I can't hold you,
Yet too foolish to let you go.

Pain Needs No Title

The next time I see you
I probably will not speak to you
Because each time I see you
I hurt.
From loving you too much.
So to avoid the hurt... I probably just
Won't see you.

Love Redefined

It was not about feeling great
Or "extremely excited" anymore.
And it hardly had anything to do with
Fantasies, romance, what was
Fashionable or Fictional.
Rather, it was all about being
Close, safe, and secure.
Comfortable, satisfied, and
Completely in control.
It was about a rare pleasure
A special joy in sharing my life with you.
It was what some call love…
What I call: Life Meant to Be.

More

The miles threatened to distance us
But that was impossible for you and me.
What we shared we called love.
But it was more.
It was long-lasting,
But it was more.
It was pleasure,
But it was more.
It was respect and romance and
Right on time.
But it was more.
It was kinship, friendship,
A mutual love for life....
That kept us together
When miles
Threatened to
Keep us apart.

Quick Fixes

It was over before it started, we both were obviously
Broken-hearted, Thought a quick fix would fix things
Quick. It didn't. Two wrongs ain't never made a right.

Einstein & Frankenstein — On Love

Yes, I loved you when I knew damned well
That you were not good for me.
You even told me yourself…
In so many words
And far too many actions.
Which always did and I suppose
Always will speak louder than words.
It shouldn't have taken a rocket scientist,
Einstein, or Frankenstein to make
Me see just how bad you were for me.
It shouldn't have.
So where is this Dr. Frankenstein when you need him?
Cause I loved you even when I knew damn well
I shouldn't.

Letting Go

I saw you last week,
I wanted to touch you
To hold you, to speak.
But something in me said, "No."
No. Something said this time you must let go.
When I saw you memories flooded my mind,
The good times, the love I found hard to leave behind.
It all flashed before me, I wonder if you know
Still the voice said I had to let go.
Yes, I saw you
Looking better than ever,
One day last week,
I sure wanted to say something
To reach out, to speak.
I decided I couldn't when my heart said "no."
It was then that I realized I had to let go.

Physical Fitness: Poetic Exercise for the Heart

Loving , Hurting, and Loving Even More

Loving you was not supposed to hurt,
Feel bad,
Or make me cry, you know…..
But it does. Sometimes I even want to die.
Loving you was never supposed to cause such pain.
But it sure as Hell does.
And I still keep on loving you.

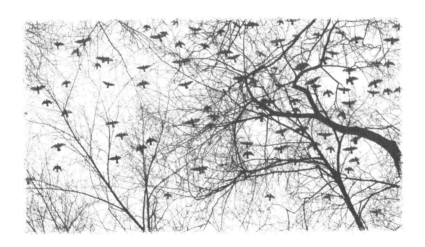

In Thin Air

Something happened to the love we shared
It just disappeared in thin air.
Our love was there was one minute…gone the next.
Somebody must've fixed our love
Must'a been a hex.
Cause we had a good love,
A real love,
A love that was supposed to stand
The test of time.
But it didn't.
For the longest we both knew it was there,
Then all of a sudden it was gone—
Just like that
In thin air.

Too Much Distance, Not Enough Time

Who would have thought our love would fall victim
to distance and time?
The brief moments we stole were precious for
grand reunions time after time.
And certainly absence made the heart grow fonder—
At least that's what they always said.
Yet, somehow, time —- once our ally — became our foe,
Using tactics we didn't know.
Time took its toll on the good times we thought would never end,
The battle was over before it began.
A handicap distance was never thought to be
Before, it had provided space and tenacity.
Looking back there was too much distance,
Not enough time,
But at some point one must stop and truly wonder
Can absence always make the heart grow fonder?
Ideally yes, but really no…
So time took its toll. And time and distance and a sneak attack
Leave us victims with little means of fighting back.
Who would've guessed our battalion was without might?
That the front lines would go down without a fight.
But time and distance could not be beat
We have no choice but to accept defeat.

A Love Revelation

I loved you much more than I loved myself,
Otherwise I wouldn't have allowed you to "put me on the shelf,"
I wouldn't have been "saved for a rainy day,"
Cast aside, ignored or simply tossed away.

If I had loved me as much as I loved you,
The things you did to me would have been done back to you.
But I was too much in love to ever do you wrong,
And with each insult you gave me — I just went right along.....
Loving you and loving you more
Than I could ever love myself.
Settling for any little bit
Of your love that was left.
Thank God I've actually learned to love me,
Which is really the way God intended for it to be.

Just Because I Guess

The fire was put out, smothered,
The ashes were watered down—
Though it wasn't your fire.
You were neither cold nor hot!!
It wasn't your fire that you put out.
I guess for you—
It was just something to do.

My Foolish Ways

I want to pick my phone up
And call you and make what
I know will be a complete
Fool of myself.
Because I know another woman will
Answer again like so many times before
When I made a complete fool
Of myself by
Thinking of you
And being bold if not outright
Beside myself by dialing your number....
Maybe if I write a
Poem about my foolish ways
I'll save myself the embarrassment
Of hearing her say in so many ways
That you're busy and can't come to the phone.
Maybe that's what I need
When I'm all alone and about
To make
A complete fool of myself.

Doing Without You

*I suppose I've learned to do without you,
I've done "without" you so many times....
Even times I thought I could never do without you,
You forced the issue,
You would not come,
You would not call,
I finally learned after all
That I could in fact do "without" you.
It doesn't mean I love you any less
Or think that it is best,
You forced the issue with no regrets
I simply have to do "without" you.*

Necessary Needs

I feel a need tonight to be held and squeezed real tight
I want to be told that everything's goin' to be all right,
Wrapped in someone's arms all through the night,
And loved, caressed, recelebrated, which isn't a word at all....
Just a feeling that is out of this world when I am held all night
And squeezed tight and made to feel that
Everything's all right.

His Eyes

It was all in his eyes....
I couldn't quite tell what it was
Or why he made me feel so good
But I was somebody
When I looked into his eyes
I was loved and I felt brand new.

A Certain Feeling On A Certain Day……

On days like this I think of you,
And the wild and wonderful things you do….
To me….
I think of the quiet moments we share together,
The laughs, the memories that we treasure,
On days like this I think of your kiss
And your gentle embrace,
Oh how I miss you on these kinds of days,
Just what kind of day is a day like this????
It's just an ordinary day, a day like this.

Wondering

Why did we let our love slip away?
We had been so good together
Making love was always a pleasure
Taking walks and having fun
We were fantastic when we were one...
But then one day
All of a sudden it happened
We let our love just slip away
Gone were the laughs
The hopes the fun time
When I was yours and you were mine
Our love had fallen victim to the test of time
Miles separated us but we would still endure
We had a bond come what may—
Still some way, somehow — our love
Slipped away
My heart would flutter
When you crossed my mind
A day would not pass that we would
Not touch one another through thoughts
And occasionally the telephone lines...
But one day...our love
Just slipped away.

Not At All Surprised

A one night stand doesn't bother me
I didn't think you'd call back
It doesn't surprise me the least bit that
You just wanted to get in the sack.
I knew something was wrong
The very moment that we met
Sex was written all over your face
So why should I be upset?
It's been a month now
Since I heard a word from you
It was officially a one-night stand
So what else is new?

Internal Struggles

I wanted to be "something" enough,
To dial your number
Bold enough…strong enough
Just woman to woman enough I didn't know…
It was just so hard letting go
Allowing her the victory of having you,
Though I'm sure she was just as deserving too.
I wouldn't have been cold, brass, or insensitive
That certainly wasn't the thing to do
All I wanted was a moment with you.
To hear your voice and feel the comfort of remembered
Love.
But I wasn't bold enough…strong enough…
Woman to woman enough…I don't know.
It's just so damn hard letting you go.

Loveless Love

There should never have been a question
Whether what we shared was true love.
Real love. Cleopatra and Mark Anthony Love.
Sure I was idealistic. A romantic, you declared.
Such things only occurred in fairy tales.
Be real you declared.
But our love was real.
We gave the rainbows more vibrant colors
Our passion added stars to the galaxy
Together we climbed unheard of heights.
We reached heaven and came back again.
And when we did sun and moon both smiled on us.
A fairy tale? Hardly!
Our love was very real.
Somehow you felt more comfortable though
Believing the contrary. And I permitted such.
A loveless love it had to be. Yet
We still create constellations.
We still set fire to the world.
I just don't cry out unhesitatingly or uncontrollably
My love for you in this "loveless" love.
Though the contrary is written all over your face.
It certainly isn't the best feeling in the world.
At least not anymore.

The Choice Is Yours

I am not about to beg you to love me,
I did that once upon a time
A long time ago.
When I thought I could not live without you
When I thought the world would end without you
When I thought you hung the
Stars and the moon
When I *thought*
More than I would ever *know*
Back when I *thought* of no one but you.
But I don't beg anymore.
You either love me or you don't.
You'll be in my life
Or you won't.
The choice is yours.

Inside

I am crying again on the inside,
The pain is too much for me
Is love supposed to hurt this bad
Why all this misery?

I am crying again on the inside
My heart's been broken in two
Is love supposed to hurt this bad
Why am I always so blue?

I am crying again on the inside
At the point of death you see…
Is love supposed to hurt this bad
I swear it's killing me.

I can't eat, I can't sleep
I don't even go to work no more…
I don't think I can go on
I can't take this pain any more.

I am crying again on the inside
Can you imagine the pain I feel,
Love was never meant to cause one pain
In time you say I will heal?

I am crying again on the inside
I am hurting, that you can see
I am crying again on the inside,
Love keeps making a fool out of me.

This Time It Was For Real

We said goodbye again
Though this time it was for good.
I knew it wouldn't last forever —
It had to end someday—
We both knew it would.
Too bad it had to end this way...
We said so much, yet we had so little to say.
No more small talk, no secret plans,
No warm embraces, no more holding hands.
No forbidden kisses, or fantasy wishes—
The book has been closed on what our
Hearts surely must feel....
We said goodbye again,
But this time it was for real.

Kindly Tell Me So

If you don't want my love,
Kindly let me know.
I'll put it away quietly,
And never let it show.
No hard feelings, no displays of
Utter despair, just a simple
Parting of ways.
A clearing of the air,
No one ever knows,
Just how quickly love grows,
To passion and desire.
Too soon, too often for some
Love burns like a wild fire.
So if my love is too much,
Too soon for you,
Kindly tell me so—
I'll find strength somehow to simply
Let you go.

Loving You To Death

I can only love you with half my heart
The whole is too much for you,
You say I'm being emotional,
Now that I might agree to too.
But I called it love
I called it caring
I called it simply
Loving you to death.
And maybe that was the problem
When you needed space and time for self.
I called it togetherness
Oneness
A unified love,
It was simply a pleasure for me
When you were all I could think of.
I called it Seventh Heaven,
Heaven on Earth,
And forever on cloud nine.
While I hoped that you loved me with all your heart
I knew I loved you with all mine.
And maybe that was the problem,
When you needed space and time.
So with only half my heart I shall love you
Giving you space, time and whatever else
You need, my friend, my love, so that I don't in fact:
Love you to death!!!

Tears In The Night

It is a shame
This game of Love
When I can love you so hard
Miss you so much
And you not even know my name.
It's a downright shame,
This game of Love.
When all I think of is you,
When involuntarily you're a part of all I do.
It's a shame this game of Love,
When all night this heart aches,
Knowing any minute it's likely to break,
When miles mean little
The love is ever so strong
And the love is right
Even though it's sometimes wrong.
What a shame,
This treacherous game of Love
Yet I would have it…
No other way.

A Time To Feel My Pain

To everything there is a season
A time to build up
A time to tear down
A time to rejoice
Or not make a sound
A time to be born and a time to die,
A time to laugh and a time to cry.
This time it's time for you—
To know what I've been going through.
Time for you to know
Just how much I cared,
Only to have you walk away,
How could you dare?
It's time for you — yes I'll say it
Nice and Plain —
To feel a little hurt
It's time for you to feel my pain.
Time for you to finally want me
Then and only then maybe you'll see
That without a doubt, my love,
You meant the absolute world to me.
But not once did you reciprocate my honesty,
Not once did you say you ever loved me.
So of course I am now sounding the alert,
As your heart begins to ache and it starts to hurt.
As tears begin to fall
As you begin to cry,
The time has come
Of course you know why.
To everything there is a season,

Broken Hearts Do Heal

A time to love
And be loved in return.
A time to live, a time to learn
A time to keep the faith
A time to let go,
A time to hang high,
A time to lay low.
This time it's your time to know
How it feels,
To long for a love that you had but
Lost.... A love that was ever so real.

Ooohhhh!!

You played me like I've never been played before,
Tore my heart right out and shredded it to the core.
Told me you loved me
Said I was the one. Yes you played me this time.
You must've had a hell of a ton of fun.
You played me all right by making
Sweet love to me
All through the night
There was so much ecstasy…
Then one day I looked around only to find you gone,
You played me something awful but your day
Will one day come.
One day that heart of yours will break into so many pieces,
You'll liken the pain that's felt to the sucking of leeches,
Draining your arteries, and devouring your veins
Scouring your heart, infecting your brain.
No doctor will have a cure for the pain you will incur,
Cause playing me was wrong,
Of this you can be sure.
You should have known I'm not the one,
You'll hurt, you'll cry…you'll want to
Go somewhere and die,
For shredding my heart down to the core,
For playing me like I never been played before.

I Wanted To…

I wanted to love you
I just didn't know how
I wanted to hold you but
I didn't know when
I wanted to be more to you
Than just a friend
Yes I wanted to kiss you
Again and again…
But I didn't know if you felt the same
Or if you thought perhaps I
Was only playing some kind of game.
I wasn't.

I wanted to love you,
Hold you
Kiss you
And make you mine
But the past pains of love were
Always there and so prevalent in my mind.

What We Had Before

Let's get back to where we were
When the pressure was nil
And the love was real,
Let's make love on the sofa, on the floor
Let's rekindle the love we had once before.

We can put back the joy that we once felt
When times were hard
And we gave from our hearts.
We could come or call and think nothing of it—
Cause it always ended with the best lovemaking.

Let's reach for the trust that brought us together
We were best friends, always to the very end.
Let's get back to where we were before,
Let's make love in the kitchen,
Let's do it outdoors,
Let's love from our hearts, more and more,
Let's do all we can to have the kind of love
We had before.

I'm Out of Your Life, You Don't Deserve My Love
(song March 1992)

It took many sleepless nights, and far too many tears
To finally realize, my love that the years with you
were truly wasted years.
I guess you never knew — I doubt that you ever cared,
That my love was real — true to the core —
none other could compare.
So I'm out of your life now, I was already out of your mind.
I'll soon be out of your way, just give me time.
You don't deserve my love, what more can I say,
I refuse to ever again play the games you want to play.

While I was loving you, you were loving someone else,
I made time for you, but you thought only of yourself,
Surely, you must have known just how much I cared,
But love me back? Not you! You wouldn't dare.
So I'm out of your life now, I've at last set you free,
You don't deserve my love Somebody is out there,
someone especially for me.

My love was always too strong, what more can I say?
I'm out of your life, it's another day.

Perhaps one day you'll awaken and see how blind you were,
Maybe you'll have regrets when old memories begin to stir,
Obviously, you didn't know what a good thing you had
You took my love for granted, I was just a fad.
My only regret is that I wasted some very precious years,
You didn't deserve my love and you certainly aren't worth my tears,

Physical Fitness: Poetic Exercise for the Heart

But now I'm out, gone, and on my merry way,
I'll be damned if I'll cry again for you, What more can I say....
I'm out of your life, you didn't deserve my love of course...
I'll get my life together what will you do with yours?

Taking the Load Off, Baby

The Sisters At Selena's Salon

They had to be watching me like I was watching them
(sisters do this)
Assessing, analyzing, categorizing, and sometimes supersizing...
Looking at their shoes, their shapes, identifying their shame?
Drawing conclusions with scented magic markers
without even knowing their names...
The sisters down at the beauty shop.
The stories they could tell set them apart
Every other sister talking 'bout somebody's broken heart:
"Girl, I woulda left," "What did you do?"
"Child, don't let that man take advantage of you."
The sisters getting more beautiful than ever...
down at Selena's Beauty Shop.
I looked at their nails, their noses, their prayer-worn knees,
Couldn't help but notice their heels, their hose,
their makeup, their weaves.
Some sound asleep after a rough day at work
Others talking 'bout womenfolk over at the church.
The sisters will always be at the Beauty Shop.
"Didn't Rev' preach Sunday before last?"
"But why Sister Jones had to show her Ass-piration to sing?
"She ain't got no voice, poor little thing!"
"Baby sit here in my chair while I give you an edge,
"Your kitchen's a mess, you hear what I say?"
It's some hard working sisters down at the beauty shop...
"She pregnant again? Lord have mercy."
"When she gettin' married to that lowdown Percy?"
"Johnetta May passed away — she was just 56!"
Lord, we told her 'bout them cancer sticks."

The sisters are actually unpredictable at the beauty shop.
I watch the sisters. I gather they watch me,
Never having much to say myself. You say I'm nosey??
I check out the books they've brought in to read,
And wonder about the private lives they lead.
"What happened on the stories? Anybody know?
"Did Mrs. Chandler divorce Phillip? Who was that with Bo?"
The music is soothing-soulful-steady:
Easy...easy like Sunday morning...
The sisters at Selena's Salon.
They have their stories and seem to have fun...
Some get updos, buns, trims, and sets
All guaranteed to walk out looking their best...
The sisters are the bomb...they keep coming and going
Down at Selena's Salon!

Getting Over

Just look at me!
I didn't study for the test, and I still got a "C"
What a way to go! Last week I called in sick
and my stupid boss fell for that trick!
Maybe I should be the Flim Flam Man,
cause I got a great "Get-Over" plan!
I get over on cashiers, coaches, and cops,
I've gotten over on my brothers, sisters,
even my moms and my pops.
In a tight situation, I get over on my crew,
if I feel I can I'll get over on you.
It's not a big deal—getting over on folks,
I'm headed to the top, I know the ropes.
I can't help it if people think I'm "All That."
When I get where I'm going, I don't plan to go back.
My mom once told me it would catch up with me,
but it hasn't yet and I'm 33.
She said one day, I'd have to pay,
I guess she's talking 'bout the Judgment Day.
But I don't think so... besides quitting would be hard,
I've gotten so good, yeah, I 'spect I can get over on God.
In case I don't and Hell is where I go,
Folks, I'll be the last
to say I didn't know.

A "Kept" Woman

I want to be a woman "kept,"
Loved and adored
Bedecked in diamonds, draped in furs
Protected by shield and sword!

As a woman "kept" I will be pampered from head to toe,
Read to and cherished too,
Escorted just for show.

It's not strange that I should wish to be treated like a queen,
I'm worth the fuss and then some,
No matter how vain it seems.

I'd do my share of loving you and giving you your due,
I'd always be the one that waits with open arms for you!

I'm good with conversation
Planning, private and public relations
Supporting and preparing
And pushing human relations,
Sure I can cook although I don't
It isn't an impossibility....but would we have time for cooking?
If loving is what you seek?

Think about your wants and needs
The dreams that cross your mind....
If a "kept" woman fits your life,
This is one to "keep"
And not too hard to find.

Do You Know???

Do you know what it's like not to argue, fuss,
Fight, pout, shout, scream, dream of quiet?
Pray for peace, beg for forgiveness,
Forgive — forgive
But dare forget? What it's
Like not to walk in another's shadow, constantly take
Another's advice, live by the rules of another's
Life? Do you know what it's like??

You poor married soul.

My X, My Ace, My Deuce and Three Quarters Yet

The Judge, life, and bitter circumstances
X'ed you right out of my being,
Once you were everything to me,
I loved you. Lived you. Was you
If and when I could be.
But times sure got tough,
And we got caught in some heavy stuff.
I could handle no more than you,
Before we knew it we were through.
Time erased all memories of saying "I do."
And the "hell" with "till death do us part,"
Cause that could be arranged too
If it were necessary.
But thank God it wasn't.
We signed on the line. On time.
Xactly. Xpediously. Excited? Not really—
Not about having you X'ed from my being,
After all you were My Ace, My King,
My Deuce and Three Quarters you know.

Or Is It?

When you failed to call, it didn't surprise me....
That's the way it goes...
And this is not a poem about to
Be turned into a song to be
Played on somebody's favorite
R&B, Blues, or
Country-Western station.
Cause I refuse to be a victim,
Even though it is obvious I was used
I know I wasn't confused
Nor was I abused by
Your Neanderthal attempt at loving me....
Or pretending to love me....
If only for one night.
Love ain't never been right,
In the poems I seem to write....
I'll chalk this up to experience too,
Like the last one who acted like you,
Loving me for a moment
And leaving me for a lifetime,
I still say this is not a poem about to
Be turned into a song to be
Played late at night....
That's just the way it goes...
Sometimes the better love is.....
The less it is right!

The Lie You Told Last Night
Country and Western Song

I kind of wanted to apologize
For the times that I'd told you lies,
But how could I ask for forgiveness
For my occasional acts of recklessness?

Then the tables turned just a bit
And I knew it the moment you began to speak
The lie you told me last night
Was the same lie I told last week.
I'm working late, my mother's here,
The dog is sick, he drank my beer.
It couldn't be helped, be patient dear,
I would have called, I meant to write,
The lies I told, they weren't right.

And I knew it the minute you began to speak:
The lie you told me last night,
Is the same lie I told last week.

The car broke down, I was visiting the sick
I was in church, I was playing cards with Vic
My beeper was off, my phone was dead
You act like you don't believe a word I said.

I recognized the lines when you began to speak,
The lie you told last night — is the same
Lie I told last week.

Taking the Load Off, Baby

I thought I was smooth, in fact slick,
"What do you mean? I don't look sick??"
Am I hearing the same lie I told last week?
Even though I'm sorry there's no need for me to apologize,
The truth speaks clearly, I have been jive.
   The lie you told me last night is
   The same lie I told last week....
   No need for me to apologize,
   The lie you told me last night
   Is the same lie I told last week.

Why Must We Lie?

Why must we lie?
Is it human nature?
Or learned behavior?
"We don't all lie," I lied
When asked.
Lies in my own mind
Were forming quite fast.
Besides since when did "Truth"
One's freedom guarantee?
With all honesty,
I gave it some thought.
Perhaps the truth was sincerely sought.
It is human nature,
Indeed it is learned behavior,
We lie to save face
We lie for protection
We lie to get money
We lie to win elections,
We lie to get out of things,
And we lie to get in,
We lie to ourselves,
We lie to our friends,
We lie to gain favors,
We lie to win love,
Some lies we're not always
Even aware or conscious of.
We lie as children
As teens, as adults,
We lie, we lie,

It's just a part of us.
Know ye the truth and the truth will set you free,
Since when did "Truth" one's freedom guarantee?
Besides the truth has broken many a heart
Caused the loved and lovers to completely
Come apart.
Because the truth they wanted to hear,
But the truth does hurt quite often my dear.
So we lie to protect the innocent and the guilty alike,
Lying is just a part of everyday life.

The Truth Is...

Do you really want to know if you've caused me any pain...
You must be joking friend or are you simply insane?
We haven't talked for days or made love in a month,
I'd say our love is lacking more than a little "umph!!"
And you ask me if you've caused my heart to ache—
Excuse me while I lie: "No, for heaven's sake."
Your absence is excusable,
Your reasons I'm sure are good,
If you could have been here, darling,
I know you surely would've.
Do you really want to know if you've caused me any pain...
You must be joking friend or are you simply insane?
If I didn't need you in my life I'd say,
Emotions do get in the way...
Let's just be friends....my dear
And I'm sure you know someone else would be here.
And then you got the nerve to ask if you've
Contributed to my Unhappiness
Excuse me once again — "Of course not, I feel so blessed
To have you in my life any amount of time I can,
You're worth the wait you know
I'd never make demands — I want our love to grow."
Oh what lies we're quick to tell,
What games we play each day,
Would "Go to Hell!" be too strong,
That's really what I want to say.
Have you caused me heartache?
Have you caused me pain?
Yes indeed my lovely one,
But never, never again.

Don't Come Here With That

I'm sure your excuse is a good one,
Why you didn't come or call,
The car broke down, the dog was sick
I think I've heard them all.
Whatever it is you have to say,
I'm sure you'll have it down pat,
So let me save you time and tears,
Baby don't come here with that.

Don't tell me how you meant to—
And how you tried and tried....
Was goin' to, attempted to....
Too many times you've lied and lied.

You've got your excuses to an art,
That is a known fact —
So let me save you time and tears, baby
Don't come here with that.

You can tell the biggest lies,
About how you miss me,
What love you have — what memories
And how you want to hold and kiss me.
But you've got more excuses than Guinness has facts,
More lies than Mr. Kangol has hats.

As much as you try to sound sincere
I've heard every one of them, Dear
So let me save you some time and some tears....

Broken Hearts Do Heal

Baby don't come here with that.
I've heard the lies, I've seen the tears,
Man you've wasted them over the years,
Save it — Baby my darling Dear,
Honey don't come here with that.

Mad as Hell

I wasn't just hurt,
I was infuriated
Which goes to show you
I was cause I never even
Use words like that.
I'm not even sure if I
Spelled it correctly,
And just in case you think
You have to look it
Up in Webster,
Don't bother:
I was what you might say
Mad As Hell!!
But I'll get over it
I always do,
Someone else will come along
And I'll forget about you,
Someone whose touch will be…
Maybe not as exciting
Someone who'll find my fire
Harder to ignite,
Someone who perhaps won't
Ever hold a candle to you.
But I'll get over it I always do!!!

Gutterland

So welcome to Gutterland....
Where you can be and do whatever you plan.
Your imagination runs free
Your dreams are unlimited
Your wishes are granted
If your heart can stand it....
In Gutterland there is nothing to fear
You hear what your dirty mind allows you to hear
Cleanliness is not a virtue
Nothing is sterile on the streets
You just go with the flow
And let your heart skip some beats....
There's no mayor, no council, no jail to be
Locked in,
Nothing you think of should be amazing, offensive...or
Shocking ....
Everyone is equally down in the gutter....
Thinking as they want to — listening to the mutter
Getting caught up in the fantasy,
Getting down with the lust,
Dreaming, and hoping, and banking on trust....
In Gutterland....
Where you can think what you want to
Do as you please....
It's a very warm place
With no winter freeze....
No frigid temps, no possessive pimps,
Just imagination
And total elation...

Stay as long as you like
Come anytime (maybe)
Gutterland welcomes your
Filthy Mind...

Like A Man

I've become so much like a man,
Baby, you'll be in love with me,
But to me you'll just be another
One night stand.
I've become so much like a man,
I'll take your number with no intentions
Of ever calling you.
Damn, I'm so much like a man now
There's no telling what dirt I'm likely to do.
I've become so much like a man, I lie and I cheat
And every night I'm in the club,
looking for foolish meat.
I'm so much like a man
I don't know the difference
Between right and wrong,
And the last place I want to go
Is that place YOU call home.
I've become so much like a man
I'll stand you up for dates,
And when it comes to waiting
It'll be you who waits and waits.
I can see why you don't love me,
You can't you see…
Cause I've become so much like a man,
That when you look in my eyes, mister,
It's yourself you see.

Not So Great Expectations

Women keep expecting their men to do right,
That even the one that they cheated with will come home at night,
Women keep telling themselves that "this" one is not a dog,
That the prince she is loving tonight — In the morning won't be a frog.
They keep getting confused about the promises men make,
Hoping that they can change him when he does
more than she can take.
Women keep falling for the same worn out lines,
With daily disappointments, getting their feelings hurt time after time.
What makes a woman vulnerable, only God knows,
Generally, her intuition guides her from her head to her toes,
But still she falls prey to the dog — and the wolf too
Even when he tells her that he is canine through and through.
This time it will be different, I'll treat him like a king,
He won't make a fool of me, cause I am his queen.
Oh he used to be that way you know he isn't anymore,
It's ridiculous how she kids herself as he walks right out the door.
One day some of us will wake up and maybe we'll smell the coffee
We'll jump ship and leave him there the minute things get rocky,
We'll have to one day come to our senses and
know that the man ain't right,
If he cheated on his wife when he was seeing you, don't expect him to
come home at night.
In case you didn't hear, and you somehow can't understand,
Remember ladies listen close when he says a man will be a man,
He already told you about the dog in him and his need
to chase the cat,
What more do you need, why put yourself through that...
Wake up and smell the coffee, and look at history,
The man can't help himself when he causes misery.

Broken Hearts Do Heal

But you can overcome the pain, you don't have to hurt....
Just take that puppy to the pound the minute he starts to
Scratch around in dirt.

The Things We Do....and Don't

There are lots of things we do
— that we shouldn't,
Things we 'd like to do but won't.
A zillion things we can and could do
So many things we should do—but don't.

We'll fix our cars, and fix our hair
And our nails must get done,
How dare the roof leak,
Or our lawns not be neat—
We'll even proclaim our work to be fun—
But when it comes to fixing us —our hearts
and our minds—
The time remaining too often is none.

We'll go to meetings with our beepers
All beeping—
And our cell phones ring
Off the hook—But when it comes to our
Health, our welfare and happiness—
Some of us dare even to look.
We should get annual check ups
Including those from the neck up
But we procrastinate until it's too late
And suddenly "Wait!" ....
our cardiovascularneuro-
Ventricularmuscularall-toohuman-notmadeinJapan
But by God's own hands
One of a kind, no assemblyline

Body— backs up.
Then we back down, and don't make a sound
While thinking of what we could have should
Have done....
But didn't.
"......Hello is Dr. Help Me available on Tuesday...9 a.m.?
Great...."

Time Just Ain't The Same

Time Just Ain't The Same,
even with microwaves, and instant grits,
and overnight rises to fame...
We used to have time on our hands
But time just ain't the same.
We've got beepers and cell phones
the Internet,
Email, eshopping, elove,
Everything but time on our hands even though
These are timesavers I am speaking of.
No time for walks in the woods
No time for fun and games,
No time for taking the time anymore
Time just ain't the same.
We have faster cars,
And drive through food,
Our surgery is laser quick,
We've got insurance plans and HMOs
But some still die before they know they're sick.
We've got dishwashers,
and garbage disposals,
Disposable diapers,
Clothes, all faddish trends,
Disposable cameras,
Contacts, and stitches,
Even disposable friends.
No time anymore, it's really a shame,
No time for anything,
Time just ain't the same, my friend...

When's the last time you heard a bird sing?
No time for neighbors
No time for prayer
No time for bended knees,
No time for thank you, I'm sorry,
No time to just say please.
Did you have time to read this poem?
Or were you rushing just like me?
Time just ain't the same I know....
As today becomes history.

Terry's Response:

I read a poem, the words rang true
About the things, that we all do.
About this life, we're leading here
About the way that "E" means care.
The things we do and use and feel
Are not alive and not really real,
Unless the word and thought and deed
Are fronted by "E," and wrapped in speed.
Reggie Clark has sent a call
With a poem she wrote which tells it all.
She talks about life and talks about "E"
That life is an E-word, a terrible deed.
E is the culprit and E is the speed.
Now before us we see E-mail,
E-love, E-Sex and even E-Bail.
We have E-food, can order deluxe
We have E-thought, E-auction, even E-Tux.
The kids speak E-language and are happy as hell —
The old folks just look and damn them to hell.
We travel a road of cyber E-need.
E-Kiss, E-Cry, E-cramp, E-bleed.
And all around us, we know how speed kills
The E-bug insulates like taking a pill.
The "E" stands for change, undeniably true
But is "E" what we need, what we must do?
Join in the rush and just say me too?
Or should we like Reggie, slow down and survive,
Feeling our pulses, feeling alive.
Talking to friends and reading a book,
Slowing the speed, baiting a hook.

Getting together, a personal thing.
And see just what joy, closeness can bring.

By Terry Stratton

Healing: The Bitter Can Sometimes Be Very Sweet!!

Tears of Joy

Making love tenderly
Reaching
Feeling
Teaching
Healing wounds from years gone by.
Soothing, smoothing, cruising
Reaching for the sky.
Putting the mind at ease
While the heart races by
Guiding the body to unknown ecstasy.
Making love tenderly
Making love gentle — ly
Healing wounds from years gone by
Drying tears they never
thought they would cry.

Special Attraction

Their's was a special attraction from the moment they met,
Though miles apart, there would surely be an
ecstatically touched chain reaction.
The interactions always innocent, uninvolved, and unintentional,
His voice was always mellow
Reflecting the disposition of a rather gentle fellow,
She was smooth and went with the flow.
Not really wondering or caring where this would go.
Then all too soon the fires would begin,
The distance that had protected them soon came to an end,
Face to face now what would they do?
Would either act on what their hearts secretly knew?
Could either give in to such an affair?
Was this something either one's life could bear?
The answer to the question one may never know,
But with such special attractions you must
Go with the flow.

The User's Manual for a Healthy Relationship With A Need To Be Loved Lover

To have a solid, productive relationship,
open communications is a must,
Secondly, expect defective operation if there is little or no trust....
And for this particular model, the following are required:
Patience, understanding, and dancing all night
till you both get tired,
Occasional I love you's
I'm sorry's when due
Positive thinking
Moral support too.
It doesn't hurt either to jointly plan excursions
Intimate little getaways to the Islands of the Virgins.
This model also works well under pressure,
Enjoys teamwork and bringing you pleasure,
Provide instruction on what turns "you" off and on....
Over time use of this "product" will yield the user lots of fun.
Be sure to be specific in noting your expectations.
The mind-reading feature included has never been connected.
What really works in keeping up this particular model of course,
Are companionship, tenderness, and lively intercourse (talk),
And yes passionate lovemaking since it's now on your mind,
In a variety of places with no limits on time.
You will find this model user-friendly, reliable and already tested...
He/She really works hard and works best when well rested.
Your satisfaction is 100 percent guaranteed,
If the above instruction you will seriously heed.

Friendship

In this hustle bustle world we live in
What is a real friend?
Yesteryear it was someone to count on
Again and again.
Friends listened to your problems,
They wiped away your tears,
Their shoulders were always there
That was your friend over the years.
When people really cared,
In this hustle bustle world we live in.
Who a true friend is it's really hard to say.
Backs are bitten and stabbed and some are even shot
By "friends" each and every day, everyone wants to be on top.
To make the most, to be the best…
Lord knows, when it'll stop.
Friends can come a "dime a dozen,"
Depending on where you shop,
But the Lord recognized my needs
And as always He knew just what to do.
He didn't hesitate in sending my way
A friend such as you.
A friend who's always by my side,
One whose shoulder I can lean on.
A friend who goes the extra mile
And does so with a smile.
In this hustle bustle world, my friend,
What would I do?
If God hadn't looked down on me,
And lovingly sent me you.

Sunshine

To bring sunshine into my life.
I see your smile,
I feel your touch,
I hear your voice,
I sense your trust....
A friend is like a shining star,
Always there wherever you are,
Sometimes guiding,
Generally obliging,
Providing the lighting,
When the path isn't clear....
Shining through clouds
To say I'm here....
Lighting a dark trail
And easing one's fears....
This morning as I await the morning sun
I think of you and all you've done,
To guide, to light, to warm, to simply be there...
And in your own solar way to let me know
How much you care.

Always There

Whatever I needed
Whenever I needed it,
You were always there.
Not once have I had to wonder
About the love you had to share.
And abundance of flowers
You sent my way,
With letters sometimes coming
Day after day.
You held my hand,
You touched my heart
You changed my life
In such a special way.
Whatever I needed,
Whenever I needed it,
You were always there…
I trust and pray
Till my dying day
That this love we'll forever share.

Platonic Energy

There is not a day that passes that I don't think of you,
Our friendship means so very much to me.
While we've alluded to the possibility of its potential to grow....
Something we'd both enjoy...
We hesitate — reflecting on our mutual reverence of Plato
and his beliefs....
So Platonic it is and we still enjoy what we have,
Because what we have is real, effortless, energetic,
and satisfying.

Reasoning

I tried to reason with myself —
How it could be that I would miss you
As much as I was missing you when
You stepped out of my life for a brief moment.
I tried to tell myself that it was not
Because I loved you. I had not known you
Long enough to be in love with you —
At least that was My reasoning. I tried to tell myself that
It was not because you had somehow
Become a vital part of my being....
It takes time to know whether someone
Takes your breath away, makes your heart
Skip a beat or two, or if that person is
someone that
You don't want to live without.
So the reason I was missing you was
Still a puzzling matter for me.
More complicated than the
Sunday crossword....
And in my case, I had no clues,
Just some unexplained blues
From missing you...
Just my heart....just a few skipped beats
Just a little pain from wanting to kiss you.
I really wanted to know the reason,
You weren't gone from my life that long—
But I missed you something awful.

A Wish, A Fantasy, A Dream Come True

Meeting you was a dream come true,
A fantasy realized
A wish made
That materialized
So many times I'd
Visualized
Your smile, your voice,
Your lips, your eyes,
The way you hold me
Leaves me mesmerized
You've no idea how I feel inside.
How I've fantasized to be held
So close, to be swept off my feet
To share a laugh with you
To share a sunrise, the morning dew
A moonlit night, wrapped in your arms
During a storm or two….Possibly
A lifetime of love crossed my mind too.
It was all a fantasy that I would
One day lay eyes on you
But the real blessing is our meeting
My wish, my fantasy, my dream come true.

Couldn't See the Forest

If it had been a snake, it would have bit me,
Always your love was right in front of me,
I wanted to hear what you were saying,
But I was talking all the time.
I was asking for your love,
Yet what was I doing with mine?
Somehow it never hit me…
You know, if your love had been a snake,
It surely would have bit me.
I couldn't see the forest for cutting down the trees,
You were here—but I was crying: Where could he be?
You took care of me, nurtured me,
It was obvious but I didn't see.
I couldn't imagine a forest for dealing with the trees.
If your love had been a snake I'd have long ago been bit,
How narrow minded was I, how blind could I get?
There were so many things you said, in your own special way,
So many needs you filled, brightening my darkest days,
So many times you pulled me up when down
I was determined to be,
It was the forest I overlooked—
Looking for a silly old tree.
I'm sure it would have bit me, had your love been some vicious
Creature…..
I only hope it's not late, realizing now, how much I need you.

Memories of You....

It keeps happening again and again,
I think you're gone — out of my life,
The furthest thing from my mind. Then it happens.
In the middle of the night
In the noon day sun
Whether I'm bored to death or out having fun,
It hits me.
Memories of you,
The things you and I used to do.
The love we made the games we played,
The dancing, romancing, the taken chances,
All come back out of the blue,
Like now, oh, the memories of you.
It keeps happening over and over,
And all the while I thought it was over,
I "gave up the ship"
Some time ago,
But the memories of you
I can't let go!!!

Healing: The Bitter Can Sometimes Be Very Sweet!!

Your Broken Heart*

Your broken heart aches still for
A love who's moved on
She's chosen another over you,
Not realizing the damage done.
Not once did she look back
To see the sadness in your eyes,
She walked with him down the aisle
Not ever hearing your pain, your cries.
But now it's time to dry your tears
And move on with your own life
You've suffered enough misery,
You've endured your share of strife.
Did she not know how much you cared?
Did she not feel your pain?
Can't she see the hurt she's caused
By leaving you out in the rain?
It's hard for you to let it go,
And start your life all over,
It's hard to face the realities
Of being the forgotten lover.
But the time has come to dry your tears
You must move on with your life,
She broke your heart one time too many
Make that the last tear you'll wipe.
You'll get over her someday
Your broken heart will one day mend
Given time you'll find yourself
Falling in love all over again.

Originally written for and sent to Tom Joyner of the Tom Joyner Morning Show when his fantasy love Gladys Knight married Les Brown. Oh, Oh, Oh......Broken Hearts Do Heal.

Habit

You are a habit,
I'm not even thinking of breaking.
Developed if you will
Cause of the love we've been making,
Not trying to get any counseling,
no meetings – Double Anything Anonymous – either,
No patch, no shrink, no medicine for my fever . . . .
Hot to the touch,
Thinking of you
So much.
A habit I cannot break –
Because you are the love, with the love,
I certainly love to make.

Is There a Prescription?

How do you mend a broken heart?
This question I'm always asked,
Is there an institution, some surgery, a prescription
to do the task?
Does time heal the wound
that you thought would take you to your grave?
Just how do you mend that heart and get
over the love you crave?
Oh, I've not the answer – for my heart has also been broken.
I have cried many a tear, and a zillion "I love you's" I've spoken.
Is there an institution, laser surgery,
drugs, some heart chiropractor?
What is the remedy regarding this puzzling
love factor?
My recommendation is that you love yourself
and know that God loves you,
Through the pain and the suffering, He'll see you through.
Just as you love today, you will someday love again,
If your heart's been broken, yes, it can certainly mend.

Acknowledgement

People come into your life for a reason, a season, or a lifetime.
                                                    (unkown source)

I cannot complete this portion of my life's most interesting "never-a-dull-moment" journey without thanking a few important cheerleaders, sponsors, handkerchief and hand-holders, and very strong supportive shoulders . . . those who have laughed with me, and those who have cried with me.

I can't name you all but I thank Mr. and Mrs. Rufus Marable, Benita Lynch Boatwright, Arnetha Johnson, and Ray Callender. Barry, Terry, Ty, and Debra. Nikki, Charlette, Djenara, Jabari.

And you Devon, if you had not been so attentive an audience, publishing "Broken Hearts Do Heal" would very likely be an unfulfilled dream!!!

Short and Sweet, Tough and Tender.....Love....
The Epilogue

......Being in "love" should never be thought of.....

in terms of permanently.

Loved ones, lovers, friends, and foes....will come in your

life and at times they will go.....

Nothing lasts forever, and broken hearts do heal....

Play the game of life long enough —

You'll get to bid, win, lose, shuffle and deal.....

Nothing lasts forever, and broken hearts do heal.

For additional copies
and/or info
Contact the author
At JVC2010@aol.com

Broken Hearts Do Heal!!!